A VERY BRITISH PICNIC

In the series *Vintage Britain*

A VERY BRITISH PICNIC

HOXTON MINI PRESS

Cecil Beaton and friends, Ashcombe Park, Wiltshire, 1935

INTRODUCTION

If I could have any picnic – and time travel were no obstacle – I might choose the pillowy, sunlit spread in the 1935 photograph of Cecil Beaton and his friends opposite, in which they're idling a heat-soaked summer's day away on the Wiltshire Downs.

A close second – indulge me – would be the one from *Five Go Off in a Caravan*: 'Soon they were all sitting on the rocky ledge, which was still warm, watching the sun go down into the lake,' writes Blyton. 'It was the most beautiful evening, with the lake as blue as a cornflower and the sky flecked with rosy clouds. They held their hard-boiled eggs in one hand and a piece of bread and butter in the other, munching happily.'

What is it that's so intoxicating about eating outdoors? It has, I think, much to do with crossing temporarily from one world to another – from town to fields, habit to novelty and from stuffy rules to the uninhibited wild. The kit is also seriously appealing. All that enamelware and melamine; the spirit lamps and Swiss army knives. Untold baskets and bags with ingenious compartments.

Looking at the photographs in this book, it strikes me that picnics fall into two categories: the type you envisage attending, boater-clad, with strawberries and a cold bottle of Château-something in hand, and the ones you probably remember from childhood, at which wasps, sodden swimwear, a lacerating wind and sweaty Cheddar cheese were more usual.

Not many people come to a picnic for the food, though. Most are there for the stolen pleasures that the experience affords. A book or radio on a sun-warmed rug. The country's bloomy colour and runaway light – a little warbling and beeping in the hedges. Those moments when a glowering sky suddenly unfolds to reveal a spring day, or the blue-mauve light of early evening steals along the hills.

Picnic provisions reached a peak (or a nadir, depending on your feelings towards meat) at the turn of the century. We all know the Victorians had a knack for iron bridges, but actually it's their iron intestines that deserve the real acclaim. For forty picnickers, Mrs Beeton advised 'a joint of cold roast beef, a joint of cold boiled beef, two ribs of lamb, two shoulders of lamb, four roast fowls, two roast ducks, one ham and one tongue', and that before steamed pudding, blancmange and cheesecake.

Meanwhile, how spectators saw straight to bet at the Epsom Derby is anybody's guess: Fortnum & Mason's vastly popular 'Derby Day' hamper provided twelve bottles of champagne, twelve bottles of white wine (six French, six German) and two bottles of brandy with which to wash down its pigeon pie, lobster and a jellied boar's head (sorry).

At Epsom or Glyndebourne, on the beaches at Margate and Whitley Bay, and at school sports days up and down the land, the tide of wicker hampers continues. As you're about to see, the British will happily fling their tartan rugs anywhere: beside a busy dual carriageway, on the concrete patchwork of a municipal lot, even under plastic sheeting in the wind and rain. If there's an art to proper picnicking, and Mrs Beeton definitely thought there was, then in Britain we've gone full *Gesamtkunstwerk*.

Lucy Davies
London, 2022

Horseshoe Pass, Denbighshire, 1936

Cheddar Gorge, Somerset, 1934

Chislehurst, Greater London, 1964

Birdlip Hill, Gloucestershire

Carding Mill Valley, Shropshire, 1959

Runnymede, Surrey, 1960

Kenwood House, London, 1995

England, circa 1916

1910

Stump Cross, North Yorkshire, 1963

Chelsea Flower Show, London, 1980

Hendon, Greater London, 1935

Cowdray Park Polo Club, West Sussex, 1981

1980

Devon, 1971

British Women's Golf Championships, Southport, Merseyside, 1936

Hyde Park Lido, London, 1949

Brighton, East Sussex, 1960

Ramsgate, Kent, 1969

Hove, East Sussex, circa 1964

Tower Bridge, London, circa 1949

England, 1970

Bigbury-on-Sea, Devon, 1957

New Year's Day at Netley Abbey,
Hampshire, 1900

Silver Jubilee street party, Seaham,
County Durham, 1977

Ryde, Isle of Wight, 1950

Members of the Women's Institute outside
the Royal Albert Hall, London, 1970

Glyndebourne, East Sussex, 1976

National Gallery, London, 1945

Members of the Women's Institute in
Kensington Gardens, London, 1961

Regent's Park, London, 1912

1978

Liverpool F.C. fans outside
Wembley Stadium, London, 1977

St James's Park, London, 1952

City of London, circa 1985

Chelsea, London, 1942

Southwold, Suffolk, 1985

Isle of Wight, 1957

1940

Isle of Wight Festival, 1970

Regent's Park, London, circa 1920

Eastbourne, East Sussex, 1953

Ben Lawers, Scottish Highlands, 1937

Cheddar Gorge, Somerset, 1935

Little Orme, Llandudno, 1935

Bushy Park, London, 1936

Elstead, Surrey, 1953

England, 1953

England, 1950

Yorkshire Heath

Richmond Park, London, 1937

Glyndebourne, East Sussex, circa 1960

Circa 1900

Pinewood Studios, Buckinghamshire, 1949

Oxford, 1967

Circa 1930

England, circa 1950

Circa 1950

Bickley, Greater London, 1960

London Zoo, 1954

Derwentwater, Cumbria, 1960

Circa 1951

Circa 1935

1931

Previous pages: England, 1950

South Downs, West Sussex, 1962

Circa 1965

Kingston Bypass, 1972

Circa 1935

Riseley, Bedfordshire, 1939

Royal Bath & West Show, Somerset, 1927

1935

St Ives, Cornwall, circa 1965

Bedruthan Steps, Cornwall, circa 1955

Circa 1945

Jersey, 1929

Circa 1935

England, circa 1910

Daphne du Maurier with her family, 1947

Henley Royal Regatta, Oxfordshire, 1929

Glyndebourne, East Sussex, 1959

England, 1947

Glyndebourne, East Sussex, 1977

National Exhibition of Camping, Imperial Institute, London, 1933

Brimham Rocks, North Yorkshire, 1968

Circa 1930

Chiltern Hills, 1923

1939

England, circa 1930

Derby Day at Epsom Racecourse, Surrey, 1978

Longleat Safari Park, Wiltshire, 1969

1969

Poynton Show, Cheshire, 1983

England, circa 1910

1934

Wells, Somerset, 1953

Bedlington Miners' Picnic, Northumberland, 1976

California, Berkshire, 1955

England, 1903

A Very British Picnic

First edition, published 2022
by Hoxton Mini Press, London
Book design copyright © Hoxton Mini Press 2022
All rights reserved

Design and sequence by Friederike Huber
Introduction by Lucy Davies
Copy-editing by Florence Filose
Production by Anna De Pascale

ISBN: 978-1-914314-19-3
Printed and bound by OZGraf, Poland

Hoxton Mini Press is an environmentally
conscious publisher, committed to offsetting
our carbon footprint. The offset for this book
was purchased from Stand For Trees.

For every book you buy from our website,
we plant a tree: www.hoxtonminipress.com

Photography credits by page number:

4 – Cecil Beaton Archive © Condé Nast; 7 © Norman Smith /
Stringer; 8, 21, 28, 138 © Fox Photos / Stringer; 9 © Reg Speller /
Stringer; 11, 76, 89 © TopFoto; 12, 19, 23, 25, 34, 41, 43, 56, 59, 72,
73, 94–5, 97, 98, 99, 120, 129, 137, 140, 141 © Alamy; 13, 27, 39,
87 © Mirrorpix / Contributor; 15 © Richard Baker / Contributor;
16 © Kirn Vintage Stock / Contributor; 17, 122 © Bettmann /
Contributor; 20, 51, 131 © Evening Standard / Stringer; 29, 33,
47, 60, 61, 65, 66, 67, 82, 101 © Hulton Archive / Stringer; 31 ©
George Freston / Stringer; 35, 139 © Keystone / Stringer; 37 ©
Bob Thomas / Contributor; 40 © F. J. Mortimer / Stringer; 44 ©
James Jackson / Stringer; 45 © Ian Tyas / Stringer; 49 © Harry
Todd / Stringer; 50 © Topical Press Agency / Stringer; 53 © Rolls
Press / Popperfoto / Contributor; 55 © Mirrorpix / Contributor;
57, 115 © Popperfoto / Contributor; 62 © Roger Jackson /
Stringer; 63 © FPG / Staff; 69 © E. Dean / Stringer; 70 © John
Waterman / Stringer; 71 © Meager / Stringer; 75 © Dean Conger;
77 © Erich Auerbach / Stringer; 78 © Bettmann / Contributor;
79 © Mirrorpix / Contributor; 81 © ullstein bild / Contributor;
83 © Science & Society Picture Library / Contributor; 85 © Kirn
Vintage Stock / Contributor; 86 © Bert Hardy Advertising Archive
/ Contributor; 90 © Heritage Images / Contributor; 91 © General
Photographic Agency / Stringer; 93, 127, 143 © Hulton Deutsch /
Contributor; 102 © Felix Man / Stringer; 103, 110, 125 © Topical
Press Agency / Stringer; 105 © Mary Evans Picture Library; 106
© Paul Popper / Popperfoto / Contributor; 107 © John Gay /
Historic England / Mary Evans; 109, 111, 123 © Science & Society
Picture Library / Contributor; 113 © The Montifraulo Collection
/ Contributor; 117 © MacGregor / Stringer; 119 © Erich Auerbach
/ Stringer; 121 © Patrick Ward / Popperfoto / Contributor; 124 ©
London Express / Stringer; 128 © Mary Evans Picture Library /
The Children's Society; 132 © Ronald Dumont / Stringer; 133 ©
Tony Evans / Timelapse Library Ltd. / Contributor; 135 © Estate
of Shirley Baker / Mary Evans Picture Library; 136 © Bob Thomas
/ Popperfoto / Contributor.